ENTERPRISE ARCHITECTURE REIMAGINED

ENTERPRISE ARCHITECTURE REIMAGINED

a concise guide to constructing an
artificially intelligent enterprise

Andre Milchman

CreateSpace
TORONTO, CANADA

Ordering Information:
Quantity sales. Special discounts are available on quantity purchases by
corporations, associations, and others. For details, contact the Special Sales
Department at the address above.

Enterprise Architecture Reimagined, Andre Milchman
ISBN: 1541339827
ISBN 9781541339828

In general, the information industry is still focused on building and running systems; that is, we are *manufacturing* pieces, islands of automation, stovepipes of the Enterprise. In general, the information industry presently is not thinking about *engineering* entire Enterprises.

—JOHN ZACHMAN

Contents

Something before
the Book Starts

In his famous book *The Mythical Man-Month*, Frederick P. Brooks Jr. made an interesting observation about architecture (Brooks 1995):

> *The architect of a system, like the architect of a building, is the user's agent. It is his job to bring professional and technical knowledge to bear in the unalloyed interest of the user, as opposed to the interests of the salesman, the fabricator, etc.*
>
> *Architecture must be carefully distinguished from implementation. As Blaauw has said, "Where architecture tells what happens, implementation tells how it is made to happen." He gives as a simple example a clock, whose architecture consists of the face, the hands, and the winding knob. When a child has learned this architecture, he can tell time as easily from a wristwatch as from a church tower. The implementation, however, and its realization, describe what goes on inside the case—powering by any of many mechanisms and accuracy control by any of many.*

After talking to enterprise architects at the 2016 Gartner Catalyst Conference in San Diego, I realized that not only is there no consensus on who the users of an enterprise are, but also there is no agreement on what enterprises look like.

The Alpha Architecture—the subject of this book—prevents the "a camel is a horse designed by a committee" type of situation by (1) unambiguously choosing the dominant user of the enterprise and (2) clearly defining what an enterprise looks like.

To clarify the first point, from the Alpha Architecture point of view, employees are the main users and decision makers on all aspects of enterprise architecture and design as the operators of the enterprise who are *responsible* and *accountable* for all enterprise activities. While making decisions, however, employees must satisfy interests of the other main types of stakeholders—shareholders and customers.

To the second point, all stakeholders—not just the architects—must understand the structure of the enterprise so that all enterprise activities maintain and reinforce its conceptual integrity.

The rock-star scientist Albert Einstein famously remarked, "If you can't explain it to a six-year-old, you don't understand it yourself." Well, although six-year-olds of today are very smart, it would be hard to explain to them any modern enterprise architecture framework.

However, before the book starts, I would like to explain to six-year-old architects how to make the enterprise that will showcase the simplicity and elegance of the principles of the Alpha Architecture.

HOW TO MAKE AN ENTERPRISE

Step 1. Parts You Will Need

Enterprises are designed to make money by selling goods or services. To make a simple minimum viable enterprise, you need thirteen units and forty-four connectors. Once you have those, the entire process will take between thirty and forty minutes.

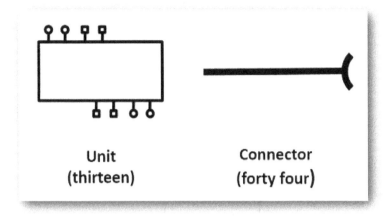

**Unit
(thirteen)**   **Connector
(forty four)**

Step 2. Name the Units

Create two categories of units by labeling them as specialist and executive units. Specialist units deliver products and services to consumers. Executive units make sure that specialist units do the right things. For this simple enterprise, we will need one enterprise executive unit and three department executive units.

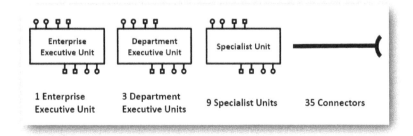

Step 3. Create the Executive Core
Place the enterprise executive unit in the middle, and connect it to the three department executive units as shown in the diagram below:

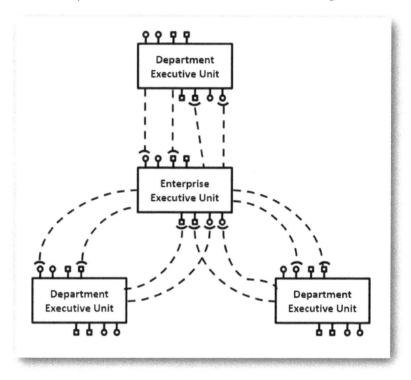

Step 4. Create the Enterprise
Place nine specialist units on the board, and connect them with department executive units. Now you have a fully functional enterprise that consists of units supported by organizational relations. Specialist units produce value for consumers in the form of products and services. Executive units produce value to the business (enterprise) by directing, coordinating, measuring, and controlling the efforts of specialist units. Note that the enterprise doesn't have any components other than units. Infrastructure, platforms,

tools, things (smart objects that make up the Internet of Things), artificial and human agents—even the CEO and other officers—are enclosed within the units.

The next and final step is to connect the enterprise with consumers.

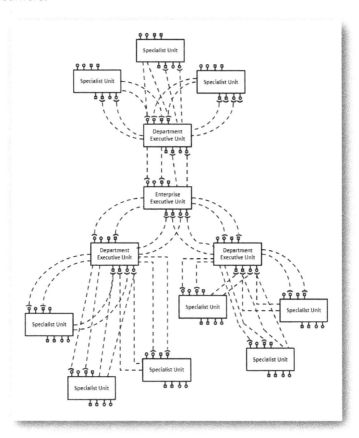

Step 5. Connect the Enterprise with Consumers

This is an easy step because each specialist unit has interfaces, shown as lines ended with squares or circles, that help it deliver products and services (respectively) to consumers.

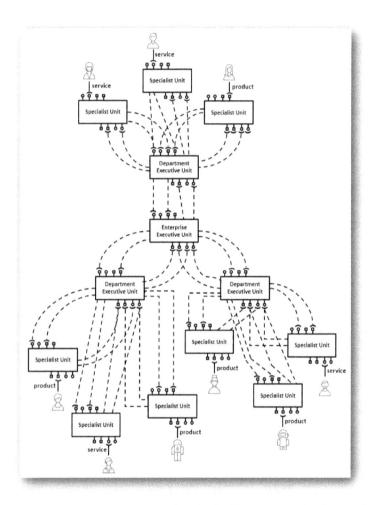

Now we have an enterprise that looks like a network of interrelated units connected to different types of consumers. For simplicity, we didn't add another important type of relationship—collaborative relations—that help units do better work by interacting and collaborating with each other. To collaborate efficiently, units send and receive messages from an *intermediator* that works similarly to a post office.

Although six-year-old architects now know how to make an enterprise, one question still remains: How to make a unit?

HOW TO MAKE A UNIT

To be consistent, we will answer this question for an audience of six-year-old engineers. Because there is little difference between making executive and specialist units, we will illustrate the process by making a specialist unit.

Step 1. Parts You Will Need

The parts you will need to get started are frame, function, process, structure, purpose, culture, storage, and memory. Once all parts have been inspected and prepared for installation, the entire process will take between ten and fifteen minutes.

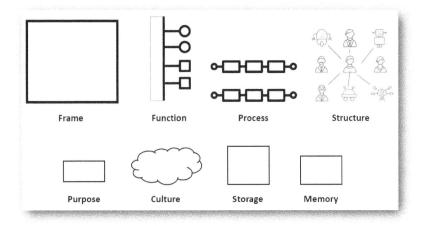

| Frame | Function | Process | Structure |

| Purpose | Culture | Storage | Memory |

Step 2. Attract Consumers

Take the purpose and attach it to the frame. If the purpose is oriented toward creating value and satisfying specific needs, it will become a powerful attractor for consumers.

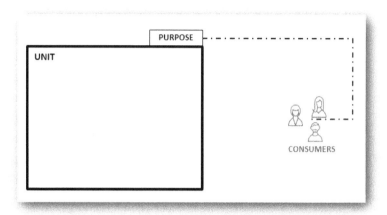

Step 3. Enable Consumers to Interact with the Unit

To help consumers interact with the unit, we install the function component, which is equipped with interfaces that enable the units to exchange products and services with consumers for money or other types of value. We also install a memory to record everything that happens.

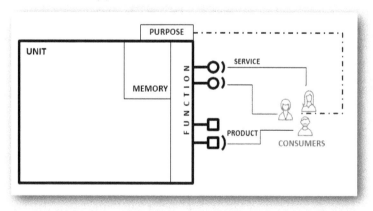

Step 4. Organize Production

To support the function, we install the process component, which is responsible for making products, conducting service operations, and placing products in storage.

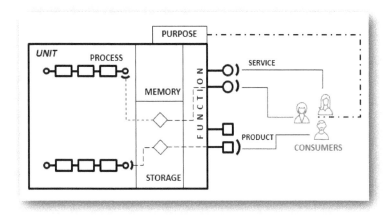

Step 5. Adding Workers

We now need to add the structure—a network of human and artificial workers—who will perform various process tasks during production.

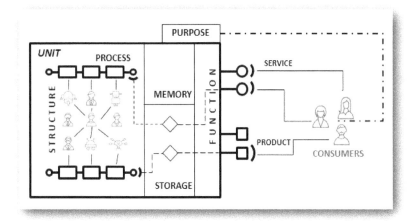

Step 6. Energize with Culture

A great culture will not only energize employees but also, if successfully extended, have a positive impact on consumers.

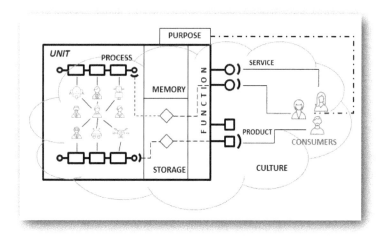

The installation of the culture component completes the process of making a unit.

Introduction

I N THE LATE NINETEENTH CENTURY, the famous Austrian neurologist Sigmund Freud succinctly explained the essence of everything: "Love and work...work and love, that's all there is" (Erikson 1993). The world's best companies have a great capacity for both. The capacity to love helps them establish strong, meaningful, trustful, and long-lasting relationships with customers. The capacity to work helps them create value in the form of goods or services and deliver them to customers in exchange for money or some other thing of value.

From the point of view of an architect, the requirements seem simple on the surface. One needs to build an enterprise—a well-designed construct that can connect with customers, deliver them value in the form of a product or a service, and get something of value back. The enterprise must accommodate human workers and enable them to perform work activities of three types. The first type is making—the manipulation of matter or material objects. Industry calls it manufacturing. The second involves the manipulation of mental, digital, or other representations of material or conceptual objects, which is called computation. The last but not the least-important activity is the social type, which involves self-organization, self-maintenance, and self-adaptation activities.

Nevertheless, to address these seemingly clear and simple requirements, we need three architecture disciplines. *Industrial architecture*, a mature discipline that is thousands of years old, focuses on manufacturing. The discipline of *enterprise architecture*, which is slowly getting off the ground, focuses on computation. The discipline of *organization architecture* deals with organizing human resources and plays a unifying role by aligning the two other disciplines.

This book is about architecting and engineering the enterprise, not about describing enterprise architecture as a practice or a discipline. Let me clarify that. This book does not deal directly with enterprise architecture domains, such as business architecture, data architecture, application architecture, and technology architecture—the domains that Steven H. Spewak defined in his seminal book, *Enterprise Architecture Planning*. Published in 1993, this great book established a process for defining architectures, but it unintentionally led the entire discipline in the wrong direction. Instead of focusing on engineering the enterprise as a whole, architects shifted their focus to the domains and subdomains of enterprise architecture. Because of this lack of focus and specificity, enterprise architects often spend their time in ivory towers and have little credibility in the eyes of their business partners.

When it comes to computation, we live in a world of parts. We break the whole into manageable pieces and deal with them separately, often forgetting about integrating the whole. We analyze but forget to synthesize. In *Managing* (2009), Henry Mintzberg remarked,

> *Synthesis is the very essence of managing: putting things together, in the form of coherent strategies, unified organizations, and integrated systems. This is what makes*

managing so difficult—and so interesting. It's not that managers don't need analysis; it's that they need it as input to synthesis.

Mintzberg called this the Labyrinth of Decomposition (Mintzberg 2009) and quoted Leonard R. Sayles, who asked, "Where to find synthesis in a world so decomposed by analysis?" (Sayles 1979). The answer to this question would be enterprise architecture. To paraphrase Mintzberg, synthesis is the essence of enterprise architecting. So, why does enterprise architecture fail to synthesize? In *No Silver Bullet*, Fred Brooks observed that unlike buildings and other products of industrial architecture, "software is invisible and unvisualizable. Geometric abstractions are powerful tools. The floor plan of a building helps both architect and client evaluate spaces, traffic flows, views. Contradictions and omissions become obvious" (Brooks 1995).

Presently, nobody knows exactly what the software of an enterprise looks like. The invisible nature of software creates no pressure for its improvement and contributes tremendously to its low quality. Although the situation can be improved with techniques of visualization, in order to visualize, one needs to understand the unifying image of the enterprise. That is why the discipline of enterprise architecture is so important.

In a 2007 interview with Roger Sessions, John Zachman, the originator of the Framework for Enterprise Architecture (the Zachman Framework), said (Sessions 2007),

I think the United States dominated the Industrial Age because it got serious about architecture for industrial products. We learned how to create extremely complex engineering products and how to change them to keep

them relevant over their useful life, that is, we learned about Architecture for industrial products. My opinion is that in the Information Age, it is the Enterprise that is increasing in complexity and changing dramatically and that whoever figures out how to accommodate and exploit Enterprise Architecture concepts and formalisms, and therefore can accommodate extreme complexity and extreme change of Enterprises, is likely to dominate the Information Age.

This book establishes a vision of the enterprise that relies on systems thinking, complexity theory, and agent-based computing to architect an enterprise that can successfully deal with *extreme complexity and extreme change.*

Why do we apply systems thinking and complexity theory to designing an enterprise? In a blog post, "Defining Enterprise Architecture: The Systems Are the Enterprise" (2015), John Zachman said (Zachman 2015),

IT has been manufacturing the Enterprise (building systems) for 70 years or so…but the Enterprise was never engineered. Therefore, IT has not been manufacturing the Enterprise… they have been manufacturing PARTS of the Enterprise… and the parts don't fit together (they are not "integrated").

For seventy years, engineers have worked on various lower-level aspects of enterprise architecture and engineering, including complex computational algorithms, database management systems for enterprise data management, business process management systems for enterprise coordination, event driven architecture and complex event processing for enterprise communication, and business rule management systems for operational decision management, web and mobile applications, and enterprise security. We have witnessed the progression from functional programming to object-oriented analysis and design and then to component-based development and service-oriented architecture.

The best minds have been busy tackling these lower-level challenges and creating state-of-the-art engineering solutions. Now it is time to create a high-level structure, a scaffold that would find the fit and assign the right responsibilities to each enterprise building block. Architecting a universal enterprise scaffold, making sense of existing technologies, and finding the best fit for each are the main subjects of this book.

In chapter 1, "Making Sense of the Enterprise," we look at the enterprise as a complex system, present the concepts of sociotechnical, sociophysical, and sociocomputing work systems, and analyze three types of activities—social, computational, and manufacturing—that the enterprise performs. Then we make an effort to understand three architecture disciplines and establish the relationships between them. This book leaves beyond its scope all physical aspects related to industrial architecture and focuses solely on organization and computation and, therefore, enterprise architecture, keeping in mind that enterprise architecture is simply one of the two extensions of organization (social) architecture. We also identify basic and advanced computational blocks and determine which computational resources play main, supporting, and enabling roles in computation. Finally, we explore the enterprise's relations and interactions with the environment.

Chapter 2, "Architecting the Enterprise," introduces principles of the Alpha Architecture—a new approach to enterprise architecture that focuses on creating unifying images of the enterprise and its main building blocks—units.

The Alpha Architecture combines the whole/part decomposition of the enterprise, which creates a multilevel structure, with the end-means decomposition, which creates a network of different types of entities at each level.

The organization level, which corresponds to the *executive view* of the enterprise, is architected as a network of units. The unit level corresponds to the *management view* of the enterprise and is implemented as a network of agents.

We will show how this two-level enterprise architecture breaks the unmanageable organizational hierarchy into an executive-level macro hierarchy and a set of unit-level micro hierarchies that are easier to manage.

Chapter 3, "Engineering a Unit," explains how to build the uniform computational structure of a unit, the one and only type of enterprise-level building block. This uniform structure is implemented as a software scaffold that enables cohesive integration between the unit's seven design domains—purpose, function, process, structure, culture, memory, and storage. We explore the seven principles of unit design—unity, relatedness, coherence, autonomy, completeness, composability, and cohesiveness—and show how they contribute to the coherent delivery of unit offerings.

In chapter 4, "Integrating Units," we discuss three main integration mechanisms: connectivity, communication, and coordination. In contrast to the traditional command-and-control approach to coordination, the new style of enterprise architecture requires a flexible—commitment- and expectation-based—approach to coordination. The new approach not only increases autonomy and reduces interdependence between enterprise units, but it also streamlines information flow and reduces the amount of coordination and communication.

Chapter 5, "Transforming the Enterprise," introduces the enterprise transformation process, which consists of three phases. Phase one, *differentiation*, decomposes the enterprise into a network of units and establishes boundaries between the units. This is the most challenging part of the transformation process because it eliminates human agents from the top-level network and encapsulates them within executive units—something that some executives might perceive as a loss of power. Unit boundaries create formal contracts and enable interactions between units and customers as well as interunit communication. During phase two, *integration*, executive units organize the coordination and communication of units under their authority. During the last phase, *reengineering*, units transform themselves independently, without affecting other units or their customers.

Making Sense of
the Enterprise

THE BUSINESS WORLD HAS GONE MAD WITH ANALYSIS. Millions of analysts work in various industries around the world tracing symptoms to root causes, dividing and conquering, and surfacing incorrect assumptions, policies, and procedures that thwart optimal outcomes. At the time of this writing, October 2016, LinkedIn listed 92,434 analyst jobs in the United States, but no results were found for *synthesist*. Unlike analysts, synthesists embrace complexity: they focus on the whole, not on the parts, and they explore how relations and interactions between parts create novel, emergent phenomena.

SCIENTIFIC MANAGEMENT

The development of industrial architecture and engineering has been deeply influenced by the scientific management approach pioneered by well-known engineer, analyst, and theorist Frederick Winslow Taylor and most successfully implemented by Henry Ford. In 1917, French industrialist and theorist Henri Fayol proposed fourteen general principles of management in the book *Administration Industrielle et Générale*. Those principles, which remain a fundamental part of modern management concepts, are (Fayol 1917)

- *division of work* (increasing efficiency by means of specialization);
- *authority* (balancing administrative power with administrative responsibility);
- *discipline* (creating and obeying rules and orders in an environment of mutual respect);
- *unity of command* (eliminating the possibility of receiving conflicting orders from different supervisors);
- *unity of direction* (having one plan and one leader for a series of activities with the same goal);
- *common good* (prioritizing group interests over individual interests);
- *remuneration* (ensuring that pay for work done is fair to both the employee and the employer);
- *centralization* (delegating control and decision making to top managers);
- *scalar chain* (establishing effective communication channels that follow formal lines of authority);
- *order* (organizing the workplace to reduce errors and waste and increase productivity);
- *equity* (committing to the equality of treatment for all employees);
- *stability of tenure* (establishing an environment of mutual care and trust to reduce employee turnover and minimize business disruption);
- *initiative* (improving operations by encouraging employees to take responsibility and initiative); and
- *morale* (establishing a sense of team spirit).

Although scientific management still dominates much of the thinking in the field, recent developments in systems science have challenged this approach, presenting a holistic, systemic alternative to the traditional reductionist approach.

SYSTEMIC MANAGEMENT

In 1998, at the University of Seville, Spain, Jay W. Forrester, a computer engineer, systems scientist, and management thinker, delivered a presentation titled "Designing the Future," in which he established a link between systems science and the new discipline of enterprise design. Forrester began the presentation by saying,

> Today I will discuss systems in technology and society. Everyone speaks of systems: computer systems, air traffic control systems, economic systems, and social systems. However, few people realize that systems exist everywhere. Systems influence everything we do. Systems create the puzzling difficulties that confront us every day.
>
> Understanding physical systems is far more advanced than the understanding of social, corporate, governmental, and economic systems. The field of system dynamics is leading to the new profession of enterprise designer. Methods now exist for designing the structure and policies of human systems so that the systems will better serve the people within them.

Forrester confidently predicted that "social-system design will become a recognized profession. It will require the same kind of intensive education that is necessary in other professions" (Forrester 1998).

THE ENTERPRISE IS A COMPLEX WORK SYSTEM

The concept of *system* is central to the systemic approach to management, design, and architecture.

> *A system is an identifiable collection of interrelated components that work together as an integrated whole to achieve desired outcomes.*

The enterprise of today is not merely a system. It is a complex system that can be associated with at least three types of complexity: structural complexity (number of interrelated parts), cognitive complexity (ambiguity of terms and multiple definitions and interpretations), and social complexity (subjective views, conflicts, and disagreements among human agents).

> *Roughly, by a complex system I mean one made up of a large number of parts that interact in a nonsimple way. In such systems, the whole is more than the sum of the parts, not in an ultimate, metaphysical sense, but in the important pragmatic sense that, given the properties of the parts and the laws of their interaction, it is not a trivial matter to infer the properties of the whole.*
>
> —HERBERT A. SIMON (1962),
> *THE ARCHITECTURE OF COMPLEXITY*

In the course of her complex systems research in natural and social sciences, Professor Eve Mitleton-Kelly identified ten generic characteristics of complex systems (Mitleton-Kelly 2003):

- **Self-organization** is the formation and development of order and coherence within a complex system.
- **Emergence** (systemic effect) is the formation of the unique purpose, function, process, structure, and culture that occurs as a result of self-organization and self-development.
- **Connectivity** is the relatedness between parts of a system (interrelatedness) and between a system and the surrounding environment (belonging).
- **Interdependence** means that any event that occurs within a system's boundaries (decision, action, change of state, change in rules and policies, etc.) may affect its constituent elements or related systems.
- **Feedback** is the steering mechanism that helps a complex system drive change (positive, reinforcing feedback) or maintain stability (negative, balancing feedback).
- **Far from equilibrium** is the condition of hyperturbulence and extreme uncertainty, when current norms, regulations, feedback processes, and established ways of working and interacting no longer produce desired results. This condition causes complex systems to adapt and build new order and coherence.
- **Space of possibilities**. To survive, a complex system must explore the space of possibilities, maintain the pace of innovation, find new ways of seeing things, and discover the *adjacent possible*.
- **Coevolution** is the process of parallel growth and development of interrelated complex systems, which results in producing the next generations of the systems involved.
- **Historicity and time** is the essential difference between complex systems and chaotic systems. Whereas the latter don't rely on their history, the former don't forget their

initial conditions, subsequent development, and past peaks and troughs.

- **Path dependence** explains how discoveries, theories, or decisions made in the past create a branching point and determine the future development of complex systems, even though past conditions might no longer be relevant.

Work is another important characteristic of the enterprise. Enterprises undertake various social and commercial entrepreneurial activities to meet the needs of customers, which involves work or work-related activities performed by human or artificial agents.

Work is the application of social, computational, *and* manufacturing *resources to create differentiated offerings. These resources perform social activities, which manipulate social and animate objects; computational activities, which manipulate mental and other representations of material and abstract objects; and manufacturing activities, which directly manipulate material objects.*

These offerings are usually products (by-products) and services, although some combine product and service features. Most enterprises expand their offerings to include customer self-service, which greatly increases customer satisfaction.

THE ENTERPRISE IS A SOCIOTECHNICAL SYSTEM

Sociotechnical systems combine social and technological elements that work jointly to create value in the form of products and services.

A sociotechnical system is a complex technology-intensive system that involves working relationships and complex interactions between people, machines, devices, and software components.

Defining the enterprise as a sociotechnical system is important because it helps architects recognize humans as first-order constituent enterprise components that perform social, manufacturing, and computational tasks. Not only the ability to perform social activities sets humans apart from other types of enterprise resources that are only capable of making and computing. It is also accountability that makes them unique and special: whereas other resources can be made responsible, they cannot be held accountable for their actions.

THE ENTERPRISE IS A SOCIOCOMPUTING SYSTEM

Whereas the enterprises that offer material goods and services are considered to be sociotechnical systems that are implemented as sociocomputing systems extended by sociophysical systems, the enterprises that don't offer material goods and services are considered to be pure sociocomputing systems.

Because sociophysical aspects of enterprise architecture have been sufficiently addressed over thousands of years of city planning and building, this book only covers the sociocomputing aspects of sociotechnical systems or, in other words, only pure sociocomputing enterprises.

Sociocomputing systems perform only computational and social activities.

Computation is any purposeful business, engineering, art, science, design, or social activity that manipulates and produces representations of physical or abstract entities.

Representations, whether mental, digital, or physical, are considered computational objects; they are well suited for manipulation, communication, and coordination.

It's important to note that for every physical or computational activity that produces a desired outcome, a respective computational activity is performed that records the work information related to that activity (the triggering event, the time stamp, input and output, the names of the task and the process, and so on).

BASIC COMPUTATIONAL RESOURCES

Enterprises use computational resources for a wide range of activities that involve manipulation of representations of conceptual and physical objects. They include

- **agents**, which are autonomous intelligent entities (human and artificial) that not only perform complex computations but also are capable of collaborating with other entities, making decisions, and learning and adapting to change;
- **virtual assistants**, which are semiautonomous artificial agents that assist specific human agents with their daily business or personal tasks;
- **tools**, which are software programs (such as services, microservices, applications, and mobile apps) that amplify the computational capabilities of agents and assistants and help them achieve their goals;
- **things**, which are any identifiable physical objects capable of meaningful computation;

- **platforms**, which provide the run-time environment and manage the life cycles of computational objects, such as agents, assistants, tools, events, jobs, processes, and data; and
- **infrastructure**, which supports platforms by providing hardware, storage, networks, and operating systems.

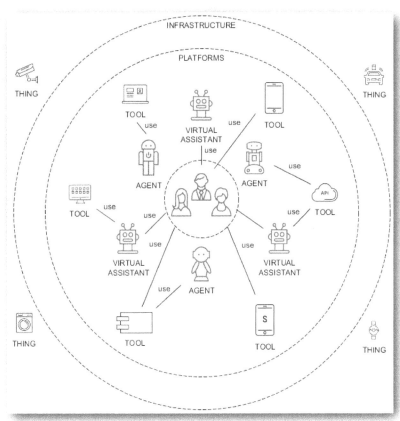

Figure 1.1. Basic computational resources

ADVANCED COMPUTATIONAL RESOURCES

Using basic computational resources, we can create a uniformly structured composite computational resource—a *unit*—that will not only create synergy between basic components but also resolve the differences between them. The following qualities make units universal, enterprise-level building blocks:

- They are **purposeful**. They can proactively identify and meet consumers' needs.
- They are **intelligent**. They can design and execute complex computational algorithms.
- They are **autonomous**. They can make design-time and run-time decisions.
- They are **composable**. They can be combined with other units within an organization.
- They are **governable**. They can effectively and efficiently operate under changing constraints.
- They are **secure**. They are protected by social, digital, and physical boundaries.
- They are **competent**. They can provide desired levels of service.
- They are **interactive**. They can connect, communicate, collaborate, and cooperate with other entities.
- They are **adaptive**. They can learn and self-develop.
- They are **resilient**. They can recover from stress, errors, shocks, and crises.

SUMMARY

We decided to exploit the advantages of systems approaches (general systems theory, sociotechnical systems theory, work systems theory, and systems thinking) to make sense of the enterprise as opposed to traditional reductionist approaches such as scientific management, which currently prevail in the field of enterprise architectures. The following are the key takeaways:

- The field of systems science led to the new discipline of enterprise design.
- The enterprise is a complex sociotechnical work system that performs three types of activities: social (organization), making (manufacturing), and computing (computation).
- Enterprise architecture leaves out the making aspects of enterprise activity to focus solely on the social and computing activities of the enterprise.
- Computation can be performed by *basic computational resources*, such as agents, agent assistants, tools, things, platforms, and infrastructures; or by *advanced computational resource*, such as units.
- Units exhibit superior characteristics compared with basic computational units by creating synergy between basic resources and resolving differences between them.
- Only units and agents possess sufficient autonomy to serve as *main computational building blocks*; assistants, tools, and things are considered *supporting resources*; and platforms and infrastructures are considered *enabling resources*.
- The enterprise interacts with the environment by providing value to consumers in the environment in the form of products and services in exchange for money or other things of value.

2

Architecting the Enterprise

"**A** CAMEL IS A HORSE DESIGNED BY A COMMITTEE" is a joke that is often attributed to British car designer Sir Alec Issigonis (Lindberg 2012). It explains the failures of designs that take into account too many conflicting interests. Somebody with a sense of humor would have coined the term *camel architecture* to describe a modern enterprise architecture style that produces awkwardly shaped, astronomically sized enterprise software constructs that fail to align with the social architecture of enterprise and, instead of being part of the solution, becomes part of the problem.

In *Designing the Future* (1998), Jay W. Forrester said,

> *Organizations built by committee and intuition perform no better than would an airplane built by the same methods. Often venture capital groups finance new enterprises in which policies, products, and markets are chosen in such a way that they predetermine failure. As in a bad airplane design, which no pilot can fly successfully, such badly designed corporations lie beyond the ability of real-life managers.*

He further illustrated his point by contrasting the roles of enterprise operators and enterprise designers (Forrester 1998).

> *A fundamental difference exists between an enterprise operator and an enterprise designer. To illustrate, consider the two most important people in successful operation of an airplane. One is the airplane designer, and the other is the airplane pilot. The designer creates an airplane that ordinary pilots can fly successfully. Is not the usual manager more a pilot than a designer? A manager runs an organization, just as a pilot runs an airplane. Success of a pilot depends on an aircraft designer who created a successful airplane. On the other hand, who designed the corporation that a manager runs? Almost never has anyone intentionally and thoughtfully designed an organization to achieve planned growth and stability.*
>
> *Education, in present management schools, trains operators of corporations. There is almost no attention to designing corporations. Corporate successes and failures seldom arise from functional specialties alone. Corporate performance grows out of the interactions among functional specialties. Present-day management education fails to convey the importance of how parts of a business interact with one another and with the outside world.*

Designing a modern-day enterprise requires a thorough understanding of the complexity posed by the ever-changing business, regulatory, and technology landscape; separation and subsequent integration of various architectural concerns; and analysis and synthesis of complex multilevel structures.

DEALING WITH COMPLEXITY

Let's review complexity-reduction techniques:

- **Leveling** helps organize a complex system as a hierarchy of levels of organization, with each level constructed as a network of elements and each element being composed of the lower level's basic elements.
- **Homogenization** creates a uniformity of elements at each level or organization. Uniform elements can easily be substituted and recombined in many ways to adapt intelligently to evolving conditions, circumstances, and challenges.
- **Entification** gives objective existence to the main elements at each organizational level and makes them distinct by formalizing their purposes, structures, and boundaries.
- **Separation** breaks the complexity down into distinct dimensions, aspects, or concerns that are addressed by a set of solution disciplines, areas, or properties.
- **Abstraction** establishes the right problem scope by identifying essential details and removing nonessential details from the problem space.
- **Transformation** alters the problem space so that it can be easily understood and analyzed. Modeling an organization as a deterministic system (organization as a machine) or a biological organism are examples of this technique.
- **Generalization** extracts common characteristics and properties from a set of objects; an example is Russell Ackoff's famous data, information, knowledge, wisdom (DIKW) pyramid. It explains the process of understanding

principles (wisdom), which begins with understanding relations (information) between facts (data) and identifying common patterns (knowledge).

- **Aggregation** enables homogenization by combining a system that contains too many details into an aggregate model, which makes it more practical for further synthesis or analysis.
- **Isolation** pushes complexity into a layer that has only temporary results. *Complexity isolation* is an essential property of the Big Data Lambda Architecture proposed by Nathan Marz (Marz 2015).
- **Reduction** transforms one problem into an easier problem in such a way that a solution to the latter problem can be applied to solving the former.

Some of these techniques can be applied to enterprise architecture, leading to the new design style called Alpha Architecture.

THE ALPHA ARCHITECTURE

The Alpha Architecture (AA) is a universal approach to designing a modern enterprise. It provides general representations of the enterprise—the high-level scaffolds that enable enterprise constructs to fit in easily.

The first foundational principle of the AA Guiding Principles is the *Principle of Separation of Work Dimensions*. This principle has two aspects:

- The three dimensions of enterprise activity are kept separate by the three enterprise architecture disciplines: *social architecture* supports the social activities of the enterprise, *enterprise architecture* supports the computational activities, and *industrial architecture* supports the manufacturing activities.

- Social activity is the dominant dimension of enterprise activity. Therefore, enterprise architecture and industrial architecture are required to align strictly with the social architecture of the enterprise.

The second foundational principle of the AA Guiding Principles is the *Principle of Separation of Architectural Concerns*, which has two important aspects:

- The three types of enterprise properties are kept separate by the three types of requirements. Evolution requirements determine *life-cycle properties* of the enterprise, such as adaptability, the ability to evolve, agility, flexibility, the ability to reconfigure, and extensibility. Business requirements determine *functional properties*. Quality of service (QoS) requirements determine *execution properties*, such as security, performance, availability, reliability, usability, reusability, and interoperability.
- The life-cycle properties of the enterprise are the dominant enterprise architecture concern and the primary focus of the Alpha Architecture.

The third foundational principle of the AA Guiding Principles is the *Principle of Leveling*, which also has two important aspects:

- The enterprise is constructed to be a hierarchy of qualitatively different levels of organization.
- The basic element of a higher level determines the nature of the level below.

The fourth foundational principle of the AA Guiding Principles is the *Principle of Two-Dimensional Decomposition*, which combines vertical (scalar) decomposition of the enterprise into qualitatively different levels of scale with horizontal (vector) decomposition of each level.

The fifth foundational principle of the AA Guiding Principles is the *Principle of Perfect Modularization*. It requires

- uniformity of elements at each level of organization (homogenization and aggregation), and
- formalization of each element's purpose, boundary, and, accordingly, boundary interfaces (entification).

The sixth foundational principle of the AA Guiding Principles is the *Principle of Indirect Integration*, which establishes the three methods of indirect integration—indirect connectivity, indirect communication, and indirect coordination—as the preferred means of integration at the top levels of organization.

The last foundational principle of the AA Guiding Principles is the *Principle of Separation of Work Relations*, which establishes that elements of the enterprise engage in multiple types of relations, including organizational, collaborative, transactional, and social relations.

SEPARATION OF WORK DIMENSIONS

Whereas *social architecture* addresses the social aspects of organizing governments, foundations, companies, and other institutional entities, *industrial architecture* and *enterprise architecture* take care of the physical and computational aspects of their lives, respectively.

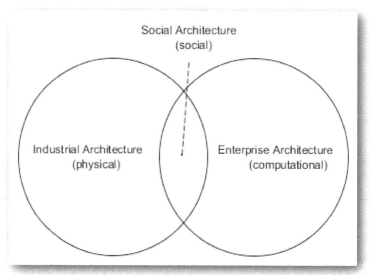

Figure 2.1. Three architecture disciplines

The diagram above shows social architecture at the intersection of industrial architecture and enterprise architecture. It represents and emphasizes the logical relation between the two disciplines and is an inherent part of each. This point can be further illustrated by considering the boundaries of a family, a basic social organization, which at some point in time might not be protected by a physical boundary (e.g., a house) or a digital boundary (e.g., an e-mail interface), but is always protected by a social boundary that manifests the legitimacy of the family as a social unit.

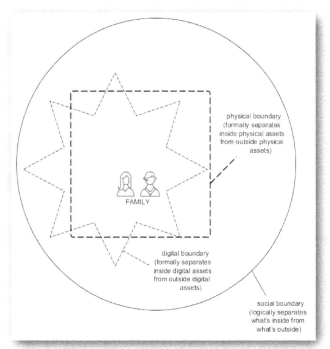

Figure 2.2. Social, physical, and digital boundaries of a family

Although it is important to understand both physical and computational aspects of enterprise activity, industrial architecture is certainly beyond the scope of this book, which focuses on enterprise architecture (computation) and its relation to the social architecture of the enterprise.

SEPARATION OF ARCHITECTURAL CONCERNS

The success of a modern enterprise depends on a combination of factors that determine its ability to function, execute, and survive:

- Business capabilities, such as manufacturing, sales, R and D, marketing, and accounting, represent *functional properties* of the enterprise. A business capability map is a useful abstraction that defines a current or a future operating model of the enterprise.

- Quality-of-service capabilities, such as performance, reliability, and availability, represent *execution properties* of the enterprise. They reflect operational and product excellence of the enterprise.
- Fitness capabilities, such as agility, the ability to reconfigure, and the ability to diagnose, represent the *life-cycle properties* of the enterprise.

In *Creative Destruction: Why Companies That Are Built to Last Underperform the Market—and How to Successfully Transform Them*, Richard Foster and Sarah Kaplan predict, "By the end of 2020, the average lifetime of a corporation on the S&P will have been shortened to about ten years" (Foster and Kaplan 2001). The twentieth-century architectures who focused on satisfying functional and QoS requirements failed to ensure the survival of the modern enterprise.

As an evolutionary architectural style, the Alpha Architecture strives to create universal architecture constructs that can quickly and easily accommodate any business capability map defined by an innovative business.

LEVELING, TWO-DIMENSIONAL DECOMPOSITION, PERFECT MODULARIZATION, AND INDIRECT INTEGRATION

Leveling and perfect modularization are the architectural principles that not only combine independence of structure with integration of function but also create a comprehensible, changeable, and elastic structure at each enterprise level of scale:

- **Leveling** establishes a multilevel enterprise structure, which consists of distinct, definite, and well-formed levels of scale. It is created as a result of recursive whole/part decomposition of the enterprise.
- **Two-dimensional decomposition** creates a multilevel whole/parts hierarchy with an end/means hierarchy at each level.
- **Perfect modularization** precisely, unambiguously, and completely partitions an enterprise entity at any level into uniformly structured modules, which enables replacement or addition of any one module without affecting other modules.
- **Indirect integration** provides a flexible means of coordinating well-formed, qualitatively distinct entities at the top enterprise levels.

Leveling and perfect modularization are powerful principles that make enterprise complexity manageable.

Although different types of relations will require different combinations of direct and indirect integration mechanisms, indirect (intermediated) integration is preferred for coordination of enterprise units.

In the previous chapter, we identified the main building blocks (along with supporting and enabling resources) that will be used for constructing enterprise levels of scale according to the above principles.

First, we will perform recursive whole/parts (*scalar* or *vertical*) decomposition of the enterprise to identify enterprise levels. Then we will organize the top (organization) level by performing recursive end/means (*vector* or *horizontal*) decomposition of the organization. The following figure illustrates the relationship between whole/parts decomposition and end/means decomposition.

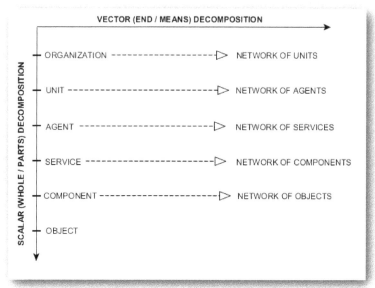

Figure 2.3. Combining whole/parts and end/means decomposition

IDENTIFYING ENTERPRISE LEVELS

To identify enterprise levels of scale, we perform recursive vertical (whole/part) decomposition of the enterprise, a process that begins at the top-level entity—organization—and the respective *organization level of scale.* It includes these simple steps:

1. Identify strong centers within the entity under consideration. The centers must be of a single type, and they must be of a different type than the whole.
2. Identify and name that type; this name will also become the name of the next level of scale. A strong center of this type will be decomposed in the next recursive step unless it is a basic computational object, in which case the entire process stops.

The following table summarizes the results of the structural enterprise-decomposition process.

Table 1. Vertical decomposition. The process steps

Recursive Step #	Level of Scale	Strong Center	Scope
1	Organization	Unit	Enterprise
2	Unit	Agent	
3	Agent	Service	Agent
4	Service	Component	
5	Component	Object	
6	Object	Method	

Note that the second recursive step completes enterprise-scope decomposition, where we first decompose the enterprise into a network of units and then decompose units into networks of human and artificial agents. Because we cannot further decompose a human agent, the last four recursive steps apply only to artificial (software) agents.

Enterprise leveling enables us to assign the responsibilities of architecting and engineering different enterprise levels of scale to different roles. The next table shows examples of such roles attributed to each level.

Table 2. Vertical decomposition. Enterprise roles

#	Level of Scale	Strong Center	Role
1	Organization	Unit	Enterprise architect
2	Unit	Agent	Enterprise engineer
3	Agent	Service	Solution architect
4	Service	Component	Software engineer
5	Component	Object	Software developer
6	Object	Method	Programmer

Finally, enterprise leveling enables us to apply a particular architecture, design, or engineering style to each level.

Table 3. Vertical decomposition. Architecture styles

#	Level of Scale	Strong Center	Style
1	Organization	Unit	Unit oriented architecture
2	Unit	Agent	Agent based architecture
3	Agent	Service	Service oriented architecture
4	Service	Component	Component based architecture
5	Component	Object	Object oriented architecture
6	Object	Method	SOLID principles

DESIGNING THE ORGANIZATION-LEVEL STRUCTURE

In order to design the organization-level structure, we need to (1) define core organization-level components (strong centers) and (2) define linkages between the core components. In "*Architectural Innovation: The Reconfiguration of Existing Product Technologies and Failures of Established Firms,*" Rebecca M. Henderson and Kim B. Clark proposed a conceptual innovation framework that recognizes two types of design knowledge—component knowledge and architectural knowledge (Henderson and Clark 1990):

> *The distinction between the product as a system and the product as a set of components underscores the idea that successful product development requires two types of knowledge. First, it requires component knowledge or knowledge about each of the core design concepts and the way in which they are implemented in a particular component. Second, it requires architectural knowledge or knowledge about the ways in which the components are integrated and linked together into a coherent whole.*

We have proposed using *units*—uniformly structured, composite computational entities that hide the complexity of their constituent parts and selectively interact with each other and with entities in the environment through standard, modular, and interoperable interfaces—as core components, strong centers, and the only type of enterprise-level building blocks.

The *scalar* (whole/part) *decomposition* of the enterprise helped us identify the enterprise levels of scale. Now, we will perform the *vector* (end/means) *decomposition* of the top-level entity—organization—to identify organization-level units.

Like scalar (vertical) decomposition, vector (horizontal) decomposition is a recursive process that includes divisional, functional, and hybrid recursive steps. We define those steps as follows:

- **Divisional decomposition** disaggregates an entity into a collection of units, all of which essentially do the same things. As a result of divisional decomposition, *geographic divisions*, *product divisions*, or *service divisions* can be created.
- **Functional decomposition** is an activity-based decomposition that results in the creation of highly differentiated units, such as sales, marketing, R and D, accounting and finance, and distribution.
- **Hybrid decomposition** is a step that combines divisional composition with functional decomposition, where divisions cooperate to take advantage of specialized capabilities.

The vector decomposition of an organization produces a network of units with hierarchical relations. The units that were decomposed during the process have other units under their authority and are called *executive units*. The units that were not decomposed are called *specialist units*. The following figure shows the vector decomposition of an organization.

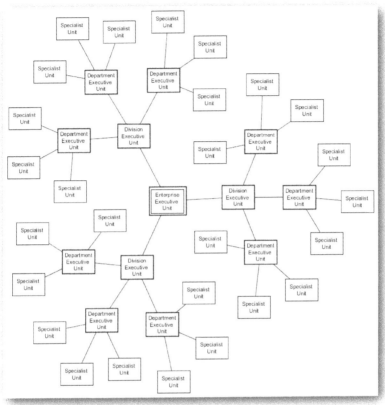

Figure 2.4. An organization is a network of units

As a result of the recursive decomposition, we have established organizational (hierarchical) relations between executive units and the units under their authority.

SEPARATION OF WORK RELATIONS

When performing economic activities related to organization, production, and exchange, enterprise entities engage in various types of relations with each other and with the environment that must be differently designed and enabled by architectural constructs:

- **Organizational relations** (1) enable a logical ends/means composition of the enterprise, (2) enable authorization and specification of constraints, and (3) streamline information processing and establish unambiguous routes of communication.
- **Market relations** enable the exchange of goods and services for money or other types of value and, depending on the side of the exchange, could be *provider relations* and *supplier relations.*
- **Collaborative relations** enable cooperation, coordination, unified action, and information sharing.
- **Social relations** facilitate and accelerate learning, development, and adaptation.
- **Compliance relations** enable interactions with government and regulatory authorities.

Figure 2.5 shows the main types of relations between units and entities in the environment. (The figure does not show social relations, which is a many-to-many type of relation between all human agents in the environment.)

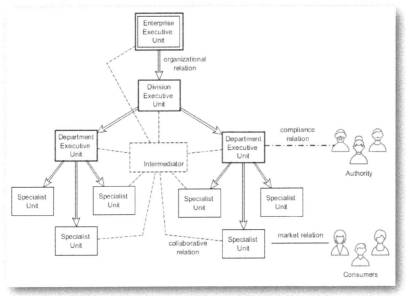

Figure 2.5. Unit relations

ANALYZING THE IMPACT

The key to achieving sustainability and continuous development and growth is building a flexible, easily reconfigurable, and scalable enterprise. The reimagined enterprise architecture described in this chapter is expected to deliver the following core benefits:

- **Clarity**. Because of the requirement of comprehensibility, the enterprise features simplicity of form and clarity of structure.
- **Alignment**. Introducing a unit as the only possible type of enterprise building block is a constraint that enforces the partitioning of all human, digital, and physical resources of the enterprise into units. Because every unit creates a meaningful business context in the enterprise's ends/means hierarchy, the right combination of various resources

aligned within social, digital, and physical boundaries of the unit can effectively contribute to its purpose.

- **Manageability**. Although hierarchies are essential to the creation and development of complex systems, in most of today's organizations, they are complicated and hard to manage. The proposed architecture replaces a traditional tall organizational hierarchy with a much simpler hierarchy of units, where each unit has a relatively flat hierarchy of agents focused on the business context specific to that unit.

- **Streamlined information flow**. The simplification of the organizational hierarchy streamlines enterprise-level information flow, which is supported by highly contextual unit-level information flows. Streamlined information flow reduces the need for coordination and communication and adheres to the principles of axiomatic design, a methodology created and popularized by Nam. P. Suh, a mechanical engineering professor at Massachusetts Institute of Technology (Suh 2001). Axiomatic design requires a design to maintain the independence of the functional requirements (the Independence Axiom) and minimize the information content of the design (the Information Axiom).

- **Clear ownership**. Each enterprise asset and resource is encapsulated within and owned by one and only one unit that manages the life cycle of the asset in the best interests of the business context.

SUMMARY

Thinking in scale, complexity, integrity, modularity, entification, and uniformity is a powerful architectural-thinking tool kit that we applied to designing a comprehensible, changeable, and elastic enterprise. Thinking in scale deals with vertical complexity and helps us identify the enterprise-scope levels of scale—organization and unit—and the agent-scope levels of scale—agent, service, component, and object. Thinking in complexity (vector thinking) deals with horizontal complexity and helps us decompose an organization into a network of uniformly constructed modular units and a unit into a network of agents.

The following are the key takeaways of this chapter:

- The Alpha Architecture is a holistic approach to designing complex enterprises; it is based on seven foundational design principles;
- The Alpha Architecture establishes an overarching multi-level structure, where each level is qualitatively different from other levels and is implemented as a flat network of uniformly constructed entities; the structure can flexibly accommodate enterprise constructs of any type;
- The enterprise complexity is determined by the complexity of its top level, which is implemented as a network of units; and
- Units within an organization maintain relations between themselves and with the environment. The main types of relations are organizational (hierarchical) relations, market (transactional) relations, collaborative (coordination and information-sharing) relations, and compliance (regulatory) relations.

3

Engineering a Unit

THE ENTERPRISE IS COMPOSED OF BUILDING BLOCKS OF A SINGLE TYPE CALLED UNITS. Units are organized into a network, where they are connected with each other and with entities in the environment via organizational, transactional, collaborative, and other types of relations.

From the business point of view, a unit can be considered as a mini-enterprise. From the enterprise architecture point of view, a unit is a complex sociocomputing system that produces digital products and services. Every unit within the enterprise begins with the customer.

Customer determines purpose.
Purpose determines offerings.
Offerings determine function.
Function determines process.
Process determines structure.
Structure determines culture.

These design time concepts look slightly different once instantiated at run time:

Consumer determines identity.
Identity determines products and services.
Products and services determine behavior.
Behavior determines operations.
Operations determine network.
Network determines climate.

Two additional design domains—storage and memory—as well as diversity, dynamism, and richness of the environment add considerably to the complexity of the modern enterprise.

By introducing a unit as the only type of enterprise building block, we optimized the information flow and made the enterprise substantially more comprehensible. Although unitization (unit-oriented architecture) significantly simplifies architecture of the enterprise, the unit itself remains a highly complex entity. High-quality unit engineering requires adherence to certain basic principles of organization and design.

SEVEN PRINCIPLES OF UNIT DESIGN

Several key principles are fundamental to unit design. They include the following:

- **Unity** in unit design is the connection of all aspects of unit organization to a single purpose. The unit's function, process, structure, storage, memory, and culture should relate to its main purpose.
- **Relatedness** means the ability to build constructive relationships with the surrounding environment. These relationships would enable the unit to have productive interactions with other units and with entities in the environment.

- **Coherence** is directly related to unity. Unit components must be arranged in a systematic and logical way. Coherence is achieved when functional, process, and structural components are aligned according to the way the units deliver their offerings—for example, via *product logic*, *service logic*, and *by-product logic*.
- **Autonomy** refers to the unit's ability and capacity to operate under certain constraints, make independent decisions, establish necessary connections with suppliers and customers, and deliver differentiated offerings. Autonomy also means the ability and capacity to self-organize, to sense changes in the surrounding environment and react to them, and to learn and self-develop.
- **Completeness** means that the unit has all the building blocks required to fulfill its responsibilities and commitments.
- **Composability** means that the unit must be easily embeddable—not only into the enterprise but also into the surrounding environment. Once set up and configured within the enterprise, the unit must be able to interact effectively with related units and with environment entities.
- **Cohesiveness** ensures a smooth transition between the activities performed by different domains and the activities performed within a domain.

We will apply these principles to seven domains of unit design to create a powerful continuum between the unit and the entities in the surrounding environment.

SEVEN DOMAINS OF UNIT DESIGN
In the previous chapters, we considered the design of the enterprise as a complex sociotechnical system that operates in multiple

environments and interacts with a variety of producers and consumers. We can logically extend this consideration to include a unit, which can be considered as a mini-enterprise that operates in a less complex environment. The composition and organization of the following seven domains of unit design determine a unit's ability to deliver its offerings to consumers:

- **Purpose** attracts consumers by specifying an intent to satisfy their needs.
- **Function** directly supports the purpose and enables consumer interactions with the unit.
- **Process** is a set of operations that are executed in support of the function.
- **Structure** is a set of agents who commit to play the roles and perform activities in support of the process.
- **Storage** provides facilities for collecting, storing, and archiving the artifacts related to offerings of the unit (the products, by-products, and services).
- **Memory**, short-term and long-term, provides facilities for recording and recalling the information related to the life of the unit, such as data, messages, events, jobs, processes, tasks, and decisions.
- **Culture** is composed of the shared values, norms, myths, beliefs, customs, and practices that energize the structure and contribute to automatic making of complex ethical decisions.

The following figure shows the relationships between the seven domains of unit design.

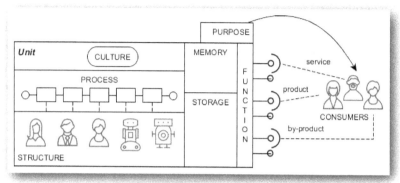

Figure 3.1. The seven domains of unit design

IDENTIFYING THE PURPOSE

Specifying a unit's purpose, for example, *tax accounting* (unit), helps the unit to differentiate itself within the organization or the marketplace and attract internal and external customers who use it to discover, identify, and connect with the unit. Purpose is the strong unifying end toward which all unit activities are oriented (the unity principle).

EXPOSING THE FUNCTION

Although some view purpose and function as similar concepts, the difference between them is substantial. Whereas the purpose corresponds to the unit's identity and the role it plays in the environment, the function corresponds to specific responsibilities and determines how the unit interacts with the environment. In *Differences That Make a Difference*, Russell L. Ackoff (2010) remarked,

> It is the way a user uses a thing that determines what its functions are. For example, a clock may be used to tell time and also as a paperweight. If thrown at someone, it can also be used as a weapon. It is the user of a thing

that has a function that is responsible for its use. Thus the driver of an automobile is responsible for safe driving. A car may cause an accident because of a part's failure, but the automobile is not responsible for that accident. The maker of the car who used a defective part is. Questions of responsibility for accidents and failures easily become public issues. For example, handguns have the function of killing people, but they do not choose to do so. A shooter does. Therefore, some argue that the misuse of guns, like the misuse of automobiles, is the user's fault, not that of the manufacturer of the instrument. Nevertheless, the absence of a misused instrument would, of course, prevent it being misused. This would also preclude its being used properly.

The unit's function is implemented as a set of boundary components; it determines how consumers interact with the unit. In *The Nature of Order: An Essay on the Art of Building and the Nature of the Universe* (2002), Christopher Alexander (2002) describes the concept of boundary:

Boundaries do the complex work of surrounding, enclosing, separating, and connecting in various different geometric ways, but one vital feature is necessary in order to make the boundary work in any of these ways: the boundary needs to be of the same order of magnitude as the center which is being bounded. If the boundary is very much smaller than the thing being bounded, it can't do much to hold in or form the center. A two-inch border cannot hold a three-foot field. In a room, the boundary between floor and wall needs more than a six-inch molding—a wainscoting, 30 inches high, is more in scale with both.

An effective boundary for the river Seine consists of roads, walls, paths, quays, trees, something almost as massive as the river itself. In general, it is necessary to think of boundaries as very large.

Here we describe the guiding principles that govern the design of unit boundaries:

- Unit boundaries are composed of facades.
- A separate facade is created for each type of relation the unit maintains with the environment. Organizational, collaborative, market, compliance, and other facades can be created for every unit.
- An inside-facing facade is created for the unit's own agents.
- Facades are composed of interfaces. *Self-service interfaces*, such as applications and mobile apps, enable consumers to find and access offerings, view recommendations, make payments, solve problems, and even cogenerate value without the help of a human. Highly efficient but less-flexible *automated interfaces*, such as web services, interact only with software components on the consumer side. The least efficient but most flexible *human interfaces* enhance the experience of consumers and tomorrow will be seen as a premium offering.

A purpose-driven, well-designed function and its effective interactions with the process and storage domains are keys to a coherent offering delivery.

DEFINING THE PROCESS

The main goal of the process is to create offerings in the form of a product or service that are delivered to the customer through the function. The process creates offerings by coordinating, synchronizing, and integrating the work performed by multiple agents. These responsibilities are assigned to an artificial agent called an *agent coordinator*. In the next chapter, we will introduce another type of coordination agent, the *unit coordinator*, which is also encapsulated within the same unit but is responsible for coordinating the units under its authority. Depending on the complexity of the work, we can use two types of coordination: direct or indirect.

Direct (command-and-control) coordination works best for explicitly defined production, administrative, and case-management processes. For these activities, the *agent coordinator* interacts with Business Process Management software, which is responsible for modeling, deployment, execution, and monitoring business processes.

Indirect coordination is better suited for complex knowledge work that is (1) greatly uncertain with respect to input, work algorithm, and output; (2) difficult to describe; (3) frequently changed; and (4) performed by groups of experts. Despite limited ability to connect, communicate, and compute, social insects were able to solve the coordination paradox and execute complex projects thousands of years ago. Although indirect coordination is conceptually simpler and much easier to implement than business process management is, the software industry has not made much progress in the right direction.

In the next chapter, we propose an indirect coordination methodology—Worknet Management—and a simple Worknet Management Notation.

Worknet is an indirect coordination mechanism based on the event-activity-event pattern. Worknets organically emerge to address complex work situations. Because the Worknet definition does not require any design, Worknets form various work network structures at run time.

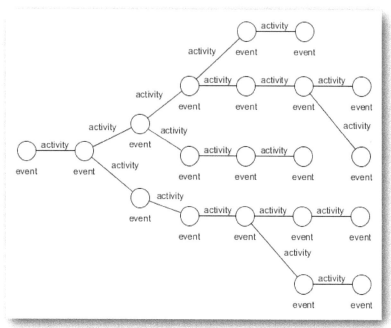

Figure 3.2. Indirect coordination (the event-activity-event pattern)

Worknet Management requires participating agents to commit to certain responsibilities, subscribe to events of interest, and publish events relevant to the progression of the Worknet.

In the absence of vendor indirect-coordination software, Worknet Management can be implemented by in-house developers.

COMPOSING THE STRUCTURE

The principles of unit-level composition are similar to the principles of organization-level composition discussed in the previous chapter. To design the unit-level structure, we need to (1) define core unit-level components (strong centers) and (2) define linkages between the core components.

Likewise, we need to perform a recursive *vector* (horizontal) *decomposition* process, which includes divisional, functional, and hybrid steps, of the unit to identify unit-level agents.

The vector decomposition of a unit produces a network of agents with organizational (hierarchical) relations. The agents that were decomposed during the process have other agents under their authority and are called *managing agents*. The agents that were not decomposed are called *specialist agents* or, simply, *specialists*. The following figure shows a simplified example of vector decomposition of a unit.

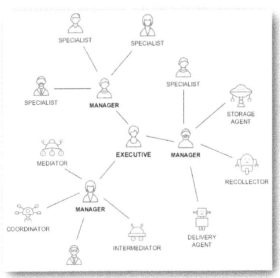

Figure 3.3. Unit decomposition

As a result of the recursive vector decomposition, we have established organizational (hierarchical) relations between managing agents and the agents under their authority. In addition to organizational relations, agents maintain collaborative relations with each other.

BUILDING THE STORAGE

Computational activities executed in the process domain produce unit offerings (products, by-products, and services) in the form of files in various video, audio, image, document, and archiving formats. These files are typically stored in the storage domain—content-management systems or file-management systems—that handles every aspect of storing, cataloging, formatting, and retrieving digital content.

Although the design of storage lies well beyond the scope of this book, we must emphasize the importance of the smooth transition of artifacts between the process, storage, and function domains.

DEVELOPING THE MEMORY

Earlier, we mentioned that every production- and service-related activity must be complemented by an activity that records work-related information, such as input, output, messages, events, decisions, jobs, tasks, processes, data, and information. Those are temporarily recorded in working memory for faster manipulation of information, or short-term memory for capturing contextual information and orienting within a specific time constraint. The most important, curated information is permanently stored in long-term memory to ensure that the unit can effectively make sense of new information, learn from past experiences, and predict future events.

The design of the memory domain also falls outside the scope of this book; however, it is important to note that the ever-increasing variety and volume of data requires sophisticated memory structures that strike the right balance between traditional relational databases and modern NoSQL databases.

CREATING THE CULTURE

Building the right culture is critical to the success of a unit. The right culture creates a healthy climate for unconstrained creativity, constant change, risk-taking, and free thought. Even the best teams occasionally run out of steam, but the smart ones cultivate a culture that boosts the energy level and strengthens the immunity of their organization by

- increasing collaboration between the agents and ensuring that everyone contributes to the success of the unit;
- declaring nonnegotiables and value preferences that enable the automatic making of important decisions;
- nurturing the attitude of shared responsibility and responsiveness to the needs of others;
- accelerating feedback loops that either enhance and amplify the change or improve performance and increase stability, depending on the situation; and
- encouraging continuous experimentation and learning.

Enterprise gamification is the most promising strategy that can positively affect the culture of an organization. In one of the best books on the topic, *Loyalty 3.0: How to Revolutionize Customer and Employee Engagement with Big Data and Gamification* (2013), Rajat Paharia describes how ten elements of game mechanics—fast feedback, transparency, goals, badges, leveling up, onboarding, competition, collaboration, community, and points—affect the five key intrinsic motivators (Paharia 2013). The motivators are

- *autonomy* (I control),
- *mastery* (I improve),

- *purpose* (I make a difference),
- *progress* (I achieve), and
- *social interaction* (I belong).

The author underscores that "intrinsic motivators are often better suited for heuristic tasks, whereas extrinsic motivators are better suited for algorithmic tasks," which might lead us to think that enterprise gamification and indirect coordination can work better together.

The 2010s saw the rise of enterprise-gamification platforms, which were first adopted by the advertising, entertainment, and technology industries. In 2011, Gartner predicted that over 70 percent of Global 2000 companies would have at least one gamified application by 2014 (Gartner 2011). Although that estimate might have been overly optimistic, enterprise gamification is advancing rapidly, and the next breakthrough could come, for instance, from integration with an enterprise-coordination technology.

SPECIALIST UNITS

Although we construct all organization units uniformly, there are some substantial differences in how they function and operate. Both functional and executive units maintain collaborative relations with other units and organizational relations with the unit above in the hierarchy.

Specialist units don't have units under their authority. Their operations support the delivery of products and/or services to entities in the environment (market and compliance relationships), upstream reporting (organizational relationships), and collaboration with other units.

EXECUTIVE UNITS

Executive units usually do not formally interact with the environment, although they sometimes work directly with regulators (compliance relationships). Their operations are focused on (1) ensuring that the subordinating units make optimal contributions to the success of the whole (downstream organizational relationships) and (2) reporting complete, relevant, and accurate information to the master units (upstream organizational relationships).

The following picture is an example of *product-delivery logic* for an executive unit, where the executive unit (1) runs the process that computes a constraint for the unit(s) under its authority and (2) places it in storage. Once a specialist unit sends a request (3), the constraint is delivered to the specialist unit from the storage through a product interface (4).

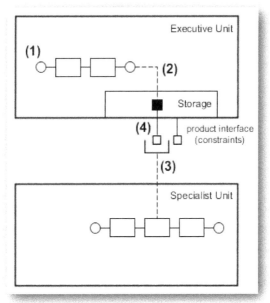

Figure 3.4. Executive unit: product-delivery logic

Service-delivery logic requires a different scenario, which can involve (1) optional preprocessing in preparation for upcoming service requests. Once a specialist unit requests an approval or an authorization (2), the request invokes a process (3), which takes service-request parameters as the input, and (4) places the result in storage; then (5) the result is delivered to the requester through the service interface.

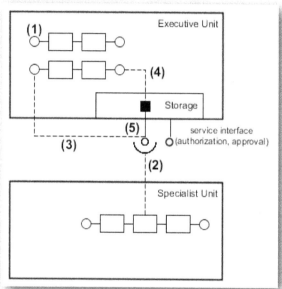

Figure 3.5. Executive unit: service-delivery logic

SUMMARY

Understanding the seven domains and key principles of unit organization contributes to a more detailed and thorough understanding of how to create a coherent flow of activities for each type of unit offering delivery logic.

Here are a few points to take away from this chapter:

- Unit design takes place in seven design domains—purpose, function, process, structure, storage, memory, and culture—that create a logical continuum and determine the unit's relative degree of wholeness and degree of life.
- The seven principles of unit design—unity, relatedness, coherence, autonomy, completeness, composability, and cohesiveness—not only complement each other but also complement the seven design domains and provide guidance on how to achieve good unit design.
- Specialist units focus on the delivery of unit offerings; in addition to market relations with consumers, they maintain collaborative and upstream organizational relations with other units.
- Executive units ensure that units under their authority make optimal contributions to the outcome or purpose of the whole.

4

Integrating Units

THE FUNDAMENTAL THEOREM OF SOFTWARE ENGINEERING states "We can solve any problem by introducing an extra level of indirection." The theorem was attributed to computer scientist David J. Wheeler, but with a corollary added by Kevlin Henney, it became a famous paradox of software engineering (Wikipedia 2017):

> We can solve any problem by introducing an extra level of indirection...except for the problem of too many levels of indirection.

When developing and integrating complex enterprise systems, sometimes we are too many levels of indirection away from being able to design the enterprise as a complete, coherent, and integrated whole.

THREE ASPECTS OF ENTERPRISE INTEGRATION

While reflecting on this paradox as applied to integration, one may recognize that if we leave out concerns related to data, information, and knowledge integration, which are subjects of memory and storage design, there are three concerns that matter most:

coordination, communication, and connectivity. From an enterprise architect's point of view,

- **connectivity** is the ability to directly or indirectly access every entity in the enterprise;
- **communication** is the ability to send and receive messages through various channels and forms of media; and
- **coordination** is the ability to organize the work of various entities so that they form coherent work structures and operate as a unified whole.

Although the patterns of direct connectivity, communication, and coordination can play an important role in the development of high-performance software systems, adding levels of indirection will bring us great architectural benefits. In their paper "Interactive Models for Design of Software-Intensive Systems" (2005), Dina Goldin and David Keil define indirect interaction and list its properties (Goldin and Keil 2005):

> Indirect interaction *is interaction via* persistent, observable state changes; *recipients are any agents that will observe these changes.*
>
> *Indirect interaction has many characteristics not present in message passing, including*
>
> - late binding of recipient: *the identity of the observer of given state changes may be determined by dynamic events occurring after the change is made;*
> - anonymity: *even when the recipient's identity is bound statically, it need not be known to the originator of the state change;*

- time decoupling (asynchrony): *due to persistence of the environment, there may be a delay between the change and its observation, and the length of delay may be determined by dynamic events;*
- space decoupling: *indirect interaction of mobile agents need not imply colocation; the first may leave after making changes, and the second arrive later to observe these changes;*
- nonintentionality: *indirect interaction does not require an intent to communicate nor an awareness that interaction is occurring; the agents may be changing their environment or observing it simply as part of carrying out their own autonomous task; and*
- analog nature: *for embedded or robotic agents, the real world can serve as the medium of indirect interaction. Observations of the real world lack the fidelity of digital shared values and data structures, and such systems are in essence hybrid.*

While these levels of indirections give us the *right* architecture in terms of interoperability, extensibility, and loose coupling, we will have to consciously sacrifice the nonfunctional characteristics of enterprise-level integration, because, as software engineer Samuel Falvo is credited with saying (WikiWikiWeb 2014),

> *Any performance problem can be solved by removing a layer of indirection.*

CONNECTING UNITS
To enable indirect connectivity between enterprise units, we create artificial connectivity agents called *mediators* and encapsulate

them within executive units. Mediators are responsible for the connectivity between an executive unit and the units under its authority.

The core functionalities of mediators are *location and identity transparency* and *transport protocol bridging*. Mediators are also responsible for security, operational connectivity aspects, such as authentication, authorization, encryption, logging, audit, error handling and validation, and monitoring performance and service levels.

Mediators interact with and control *service registries* that enable entity registration, publishing, and discovery and *service gateways* that enable intelligent routing, protocol conversion, and other transformation mechanisms in support of a variety of protocol and messaging styles.

COMMUNICATION BETWEEN UNITS

To enable indirect communication between enterprise units, we create autonomous artificial communication agents called *intermediators* and encapsulate them within executive units. Communication agents collaborate with connectivity agents and, likewise, are responsible for the communication between an executive unit and the units under its authority.

Intermediators enable asynchronous message-based communication based on the publish/subscribe pattern, which allows an entity to send a message to many entities at once. There are message providers who publish messages and message consumers who subscribe to particular *topics*. When a message is published to a destination, called a topic, it is forwarded to all the consumers who subscribed to this topic. The advantages of intermediated communication over direct communication are (1) the effective time and synchronization *decoupling* of message providers and consumers who may not even know of each other's existence, (2) the ability to add new publishers and subscribers at run time without affecting other entities, which enhances the *scalability* and *extensibility* of the enterprise, and (3) the reduction of excessive complexity associated with point-to-point communication.

Intermediators interact with and control *message brokers* that enable indirect push-based communication, many-to-many interactions, and flexible content-based and topic-based addressing in contrast to location-based addressing.

Intermediators can be effectively used at both the enterprise level to enable indirect coordination between units and the unit level to enable indirect coordination between agents.

COORDINATING UNITS

Business Process Management (BPM) is one of those technologies and methodologies that makes perfect sense but nevertheless is invariably rejected by end users no matter how much money and effort companies put into it. Although BPM is often an optimal solution for some usage scenarios, such as conventional production, administrative, and case management workflows, it is hardly the right choice for complex knowledge work.

What makes BPM so ill-suited for complex knowledge work? First, a commercial BPM platform, the infrastructure required to operate the software, installation, configuration, training, and support, is *expensive*. The total cost of ownership of the BPM platform, which includes licensing and yearly maintenance costs, is very high. Second, BPM is *difficult*. The formalization of an implicitly defined business process, which includes process design, development, simulation and testing, and deployment, is hard, and it often requires constant expert help. Third, BPM is *inflexible*. Although some technology research firms argue that BPM is a discipline that enables business agility, changing a business process is a risky and difficult task, something that companies would like to avoid—and for good reason.

Finally, BPM is *complicated*. Highly complex BPM standards, including BPMN, today's most popular business process modeling notation, encourage visual programming, not process design. The business process management life cycle, which consists of five key phases—goal setting, process design, process implementation, process enactment and measurement, and process evaluation—and encompasses numerous activities, such as modeling of as-is and to-be processes, simulation, execution, business activity monitoring, reporting, and optimization, is difficult to manage and even more difficult to change. BPM suites, which are now required to have a ridiculously broad set of capabilities, are impossible to use without the "expertise" of highly paid consultants.

What is an easier, simpler, more flexible, and less expensive alternative to process-based coordination? How do enterprises coordinate complex work today? The answer is not obvious, but it is evident once we examine how social insects—termites, ants, bees, and wasps—coordinate work. Social insects collaborate to perform complex collective tasks using an indirect coordination mechanism called *stigmergy*. Francis Heylighen, a Belgian cyberneticist known for his research in the emergence and evolution of complex intelligent organizations, explains (Heylighen 2015):

> *The concept of stigmergy was proposed by the French entomologist Pierre-Paul Grasse´ (Grasse´, 1959) to describe a mechanism of coordination used by insects. The principle is that work performed by an agent leaves a trace in the environment that stimulates the*

performance of subsequent work—by the same or other agents. This mediation via the environment ensures that tasks are executed in the right order, without any need for planning, control, or direct interaction between the agents. The notion of stigmergy allowed Grasse´ to solve the "coordination paradox" (Theraulaz & Bonabeau, 1999), i.e. the question of how insects of very limited intelligence, without apparent communication, manage to collaboratively tackle complex projects, such as building a nest.

While the basic universal principle of stigmergy is simple—an individual entity modifies the surrounding environment, and other entities observe the changed environment and orient, decide, and act accordingly—there exist two types of stigmergic interactions: *sematectonic stigmergy* and *marker-based stigmergy*. Structure-based stigmergy makes physical modifications to the environment, whereas marker-based stigmergy requires agents to leave markers or signs in the environment.

Like social insects, enterprise agents consistently choose indirect stigmergic coordination over direct command-and-control coordination for complex knowledge-based activities. In a research report for Defence Research and Development Canada, H. Van Dyke Parunak remarked (Van Dyke Parunak 2006):

Human-Human Stigmergy is pervasive. A wide range of precomputer social systems fit the pattern of stigmergic coordination and have provided a rich set of metaphors on which a diverse set of computer-enabled systems for enabling human stigmergy have been constructed. It would be more difficult to show a functioning human institution that is not stigmergic than it is to find examples of human stigmergy. The reason that human-human stigmergy is so common can be understood from the growing body of experience in constructing large-scale distributed computing systems with resource-constrained elements. Central control of such systems is not feasible, since resource-constrained components cannot cope with the large-scale, distributed aspects of such systems. The central insight of stigmergy is that coordination can be achieved by resource-constrained agents interacting locally in an environment. Two fundamental principles govern the success of this strategy.

1. *No matter how large the environment grows, because agents interact only locally, their limited processing capabilities are not overwhelmed.*
2. *Through the dynamics of self-organization, local interactions can yield a coherent system-level outcome that provides the required control.*

In the same report, Parunak outlined the basic architecture of stigmergy.

Each agent has

- *an internal state, which generally is not directly visible to other agents;*
- *sensors that give it access to some of the environment's state variables;*
- *actuators that enable it to change some of the environment's state variables;*

- a program (its "dynamics") that maps from its current internal state and its sensor readings to changes in its state and commands given to its sensors and actuators.
- The environment has
- a state, certain aspects of which generally are visible to the agents; and
- a program (its "dynamics") that governs the evolution of its state over time.

The most important distinction between agents and the environment is that the internal state of agents is hidden, while the state of the environment is accessible to an agent with appropriate sensors. In most cases, a second distinction can be observed.

Each agent is monolithic, a self-contained computational object with a well-defined boundary. Typically, the environment is not monolithic but is structured according to some topology.

Because the software industry failed to offer enterprise an effective indirect-coordination solution, knowledge workers adapted a general-purpose communication tool—e-mail—as the environment for stigmergic coordination. Not surprisingly, according to an Osterman Research survey (Osterman Research 2009), in most organizations e-mail is the primary file-transfer solution. On a typical workday, the average user sends and receives 149 e-mails—2 percent with no attachment, 11 percent with attachments under one MB, 46 percent with attachments between one MB and five MB, and 41 percent with attachments over five MB.

Although another book—or several more—could be written about the use and abuse of e-mail and other office-productivity tools for various specific computational and business purposes (coordination is only one of them), the trend will persist until special-purpose solutions become available.

WORKNET MANAGEMENT

We would like to propose the terms *Worknet*, *Worknet Management (WNM)*, and *Worknet Modeling Notation (WNMN)* as the alternatives to the terms *business process*, *business process management (BPM)*, and *business process modeling notation (BPMN)*, respectively.

> *Worknet is an indirectly coordinated set of activities intended to produce business results and synchronize the states of participating entities (units or agents).*
>
> *Worknet Management is an advanced stigmergic coordination approach that views enterprise activity as a set of Worknets.*
>
> *Worknet Modeling Notation is a graphical representation—consisting of graphical symbols, their definitions, and a visual grammar—for visually describing Worknets.*

Although no vendor products for Worknet Management are currently available at the market, simple Worknet Management solutions can be built and maintained by a company's in-house developers.

CHARACTERISTICS OF WORKNET MANAGEMENT

The following essential characteristics of Worknet Management have been identified:

- **Clarity of expectations and commitments**. Once the participating entities, units, or agents assume responsibilities and make commitments, clear expectations are set, and the entities can do their work within the context of the Worknet.
- **Clear ownership and accountability**. Every Worknet is owned and coordinated by an executive unit, which ensures that the units under its authority contribute their best to the success of the whole.
- **Minimum planning and design**. In order to register a Worknet with the coordinator, the owner is required to submit only the name of the Worknet, for example, *Order to Shipment*, and the name of the start event, for example, *Order Received*.
- **Organic development**. At any time, the participating entities can subscribe to Worknet events, perform some business-related or state-synchronization activity, and, optionally, publish events that are relevant to the Worknet.
- **Transparency**. The current state of the execution of a Worknet instance is visualized so that every participant can see it.
- **Abstraction and privacy**. Only Worknet events and transitions are visualized; the details of activities executed by the participating entities remain hidden.
- **History**. The history of execution is recorded and maintained for Worknet mining and learning purposes.

WORKNET MANAGEMENT NOTATION

In terms of clarity, WNMN may be compared with the mind-map notation: both are sufficiently simple, straightforward, conceptually elegant, and self-explanatory. Because Worknets have only two essential elements—activities and events—the simplest version of WNMN has only two graphical notation elements, lines and circles. Lines correspond to activities and drive the Worknet forward, and circles correspond to events and serve as cohesion devices that contribute to the unity and coherence of the work structure.

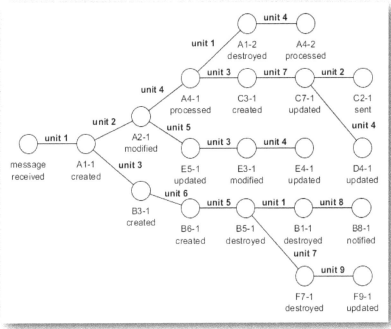

Figure 4.1. A simple version of Worknet Management Notation

SUMMARY

The process of integrating units involves the creation of three levels of indirection. On one hand, doing that introduces computational overhead. But on the other hand, it helps the enterprise achieve loose coupling, scalability, and extensibility, which in turn increases the agility and adaptability of enterprise entities.

Three types of integration agents are implemented and encapsulated within each executive unit to enable effective interactions between the units under its authority. They are

- **connectivity agents**, which are mediators that ensure location transparency and protocol conversion;
- **communication agents**, intermediators that enable synchronization decoupling (asynchronous communication), space decoupling (anonymous communication), and time decoupling (the simultaneous presence of the sender and receiver is not required); and
- **coordination agents**, coordinators that enable the emergence of complex, agile, and scalable work structures while reducing the volume of transmitted information and the need for initial process planning and design.

Worknet Management is proposed as an indirect coordination technology that can effectively and efficiently replace Business Process Management for knowledge work. Worknet Management uses a simple Worknet Management Notation that has only two essential elements: activities (lines) and events (circles). Worknets—complex, coherent, and agile work structures that will replace business processes—don't require initial (design-time) investment; they develop organically over time.

5

Transforming the Enterprise

ENTERPRISE TRANSFORMATION OCCURS AT TWO LEVELS: the organization level, where the enterprise is transformed into a network of units, and the unit level, where each unit is transformed into a network of agents.

While business process reengineering has been around since the early 1990s, the beginning of the concept of enterprise reengineering can be traced to 2005, when Erlend Alfnes published his doctoral thesis, *Enterprise Reengineering: A Strategic Framework and Methodology*, which attempted to "establish enterprise reengineering as an approach that enables manufacturing enterprises to achieve fit between market requirements and operations capabilities" (Alfnes 2008). Unlike the business process–engineering approach proposed by (Hammer and Champy 1993), which was focused mainly on office processes, Alfnes took a more holistic, model-based enterprise approach that aimed to transform the enterprise from an existing operations model. Although Alfnes's thesis is interesting, creative, and comprehensive, instead of presenting a holistic transformation model, the author used a reductionist model to break the operations model into six views (resource view, material view, information view, process view, organization view, and control view), which shifted the focus from the enterprise as a whole to specific decision areas.

In 2007, in an exclusive interview with Roger Sessions for *Perspectives of the IASA*, John Zachman said,

> *Unfortunately, few (if any) Enterprises in 2007 have Enterprise Architecture. That is the problem. Up until now, Enterprises have happened...somehow. They haven't been architected (engineered).*
>
> *In contrast, in 2007, every airplane, every hundred-story building, every locomotive, every battleship, every computer, every industrial product has Architecture. Otherwise, we couldn't have created these complex products, and we couldn't make continuous engineering changes to them without catastrophic results.*

The situation still remains the same, and it is still of great concern to John Zachman, who, in 2015, published a blog post claiming that "IT has been manufacturing the Enterprise (building systems) for seventy years or so...but the Enterprise was never engineered" (Zachman 2015).

This can be explained by four factors: (1) the failure to identify the main user of the enterprise, (2) the failure to apply systems theory to enterprise architecture, (3) the lack of an enterprise model that correctly represents the big picture, and (4) the inability to establish a pure and complete network of units at the top level of the enterprise.

THREE PHASES OF ENTERPRISE REENGINEERING

Enterprise reengineering is a complex process that can be divided roughly into three distinct phases:

1. **Differentiation**, where the enterprise is transformed into a network of bounded units
2. **Integration**, where enterprise units are integrated using the patterns of indirect connectivity, communication, and coordination
3. **Reengineering**, where each enterprise unit is transformed into a coherent work system according to its product or service delivery logic

The first two phases are executed at the enterprise level, but the third phase is executed at the unit level.

THE DIFFERENTIATION PHASE

The differentiation phase of enterprise transformation involves two key steps:

1. **Social transformation**, which partitions the enterprise into a network of socially bounded units, where each enterprise resource and asset is encapsulated within and owned by one and only one unit
2. **Boundary formalization**, which establishes formal digital boundaries around units

The social transformation step is technically easy but socially and politically difficult. From a technical point of view, the transformation is simply a recursive process that starts with the enterprise as a whole and, at every recursion, involves a decision of whether to (1) functionally decompose the whole; (2) disaggregate it based on national, geographic, product, or service considerations; or (3) not decompose it. The units that are marked not to decompose become specialist units. In contrast, executive units remain subjects for recursive decomposition.

From a social point of view, the transformation is a complicated and often politically motivated process of removing executives from the enterprise level and encapsulating them within executive units, which requires making difficult choices between conflicting priorities.

Once disputes between competing interests are resolved, the enterprise completes its transformation from a large-sized hierarchical network of agents into a more manageable hierarchical network of units.

Although enterprises of today do contain formal socially bounded units, most units don't formalize their boundaries. Six years ago, however, programmer and blogger Steve Yegge described an excellent example of executing the *boundary formalization* step in his famous, accidentally posted rant about Amazon. com (Yegge 2011):

> So one day Jeff Bezos issued a mandate. He's doing that all the time, of course, and people scramble like ants being pounded with a rubber mallet whenever it happens. But on one occasion—back around 2002, I think, plus or minus a year—he issued a mandate that was so out there, so huge and eye-bulgingly ponderous, that it made all of his other mandates look like unsolicited peer bonuses. His Big Mandate went something along these lines:
>
> 1) All teams will henceforth expose their data and functionality through service interfaces.
> 2) Teams must communicate with each other through these interfaces.

3) *There will be no other form of interprocess commu-*
   nication allowed: no direct linking, no direct reads
   of another team's data store, no shared-memory
   model, no back doors whatsoever. The only commu-
   nication allowed is via service interface calls over the
   network.
4) *It doesn't matter what technology they use. HTTP,*
   Corba, Pubsub, custom protocols—doesn't matter.
   Bezos doesn't care.
5) *All service interfaces, without exception, must be de-*
   signed from the ground up to be externalizable. That
   is to say, the team must plan and design to be able
   to expose the interface to developers in the outside
   world. No exceptions.
6) *Anyone who doesn't do this will be fired.*
7) *Thank you; have a nice day!*

This memo shows not only Jeff Bezos's remarkable vision but also the will and commitment to "do what it takes" to implement the effective enterprise architecture that would position Amazon.com to become an undisputed global market leader.

THE INTEGRATION PHASE

In one of the best books ever written about enterprise integration, *Enterprise Integration Patterns: Designing, Building, and Deploying Messaging Solutions* (2003), Gregor Hohpe and Bobby Woolf identified four main approaches to enterprise integration: file transfer, shared database, remote procedure invocation, and messaging. Although each style has distinct strengths and weaknesses, the Alpha Architecture follows Hohpe and Woolf's recommendation to "use messaging to transfer packets of data frequently, immediately, reliably, and asynchronously, using customizable formats" (Hohpe and Woolf 2003).

The integration phase of enterprise transformation relies on enterprise messaging as the main integration mechanism between enterprise units in order to maximize the benefits of indirection, nonintrusiveness, and decoupling.

Enterprise mediation agents (**mediators**) ensure interoperability between heterogeneous units by providing message routing, location transparency, transport protocol bridging, and message validation and enhancement. Mediation agents are also responsible for policy enforcement related to cross-cutting concerns, such as security, audit, and logging.

Enterprise intermediation agents (**intermediators**) ensure nonintrusiveness and independence of enterprise units by enabling identity, space, time, technology, and representation decoupling.

Enterprise coordination agents (**coordinators**) enable stigmergic (indirect) coordination to eliminate expensive initial planning and process design, streamline communication, and reduce control.

During the integration phase, integration agents—mediators, intermediators, and coordinators—are implemented in every executive unit. Integration agents direct, monitor, and interact with the integration modules deployed on and executed by cloud-based or on-premises mediation, intermediation, and coordination platforms, respectively.

THE REENGINEERING PHASE

The reengineering phase of enterprise transformation creates coherent alignment between the design components of every unit. The coherence between purpose, function, process, structure, storage, memory, and culture is achieved by designing flexible solutions for various types of *offering-delivery logic*. The first type, *product-delivery logic,* requires a production process to complete and move finished *product(s)* to storage facilities in advance, before customers begin sending requests. In contrast, *by-product–delivery logic* is much simpler because *by-products* are produced as side effects of making or doing something else, and they may only require some packaging before being released. *Service-delivery logic* requires customer input before triggering the respective service-delivery process. In addition, before receiving customers' requests, some preprocessing activities may be necessary to accelerate service delivery. *Self-service–delivery logic* is the most sophisticated mechanism of *offering-delivery logic*. It requires a design capable of addressing various customer needs, usage, scenarios, and exception flows.

In *The Next Common Sense: Mastering Corporate Complexity through Coherence* (2000), Michael Lissack and Johan Roos write (Lissack and Roos 2000),

> *Coherence is the glue that holds the organized entities (be it an ant colony or a city) together in their ecosystems and renders them more ecologically fit for survival to the next generation. From the organizational ecosystem perspective, coherence is a vital contributor to sustainability…*
>
> *When making sense revolves around a point of view held in common by those who need to act, coordinated action can occur without the need for coercive control. The group becomes more effective because it no longer requires significant energy to be expended on such coercion or the threat of it. The freed-up energy can be*

devoted to useful tasks. At the firm level, the process is similar as it applies not only individual by individual, but also group by group, business unit by business unit.

Coherence is the antidote to uncertainty. In organizations, uncertainty is evidenced by an unwillingness to act. Once the will exists, so too does the certainty. A coherent perspective increases the willingness and reduces the periods of uncertainty.

Transformation of units requires a big-picture view combined with an intense focus on precision and detail. Unit owners must make some key decisions:

- **Select the delivery logic**—the appropriate delivery logic or a combination of product-, by-product–, service-, and self-service–delivery models.
- **Choose the integration style**—a direct integration style, best suited to well-defined work flows; an indirect integration style, which is optimal for complex knowledge work; or both styles for different usage scenarios.
- **Choose technologies and styles of architecture**. Technologies and architectural styles must be carefully selected for all unit-design areas. The Alpha Architecture recommends using an agent-oriented architecture style for implementing structure, a microservices architecture for implementing function; and BPM and Worknet Management for implementing process. Various combinations of relational and NoSQL databases and business intelligence platforms can be used for implementing memory and storage.

- **Select the culture type**. The type of culture—traditional, highly skilled, innovative, social, team-first, customer-first, progressive, elite—will affect the unit's success rate and speed of development.

Once the key decisions are made, the implementation should focus on an orderly, logical, and consistent relation of a unit's design components. This will determine how well the unit works as a whole.

SUMMARY

Organizations can use the Alpha Architecture to execute enterprise transformation at two levels: the organization level, where the organization is transformed into a network of units, and the unit level, where each unit is transformed into a network of agents.

The enterprise transformation program can be executed in three phases:

- The differentiation phase partitions the enterprise into a network of units and formalizes boundaries around the units.
- The integration phase establishes indirect connectivity, communication, and coordination between the units.
- During the reengineering phase, every enterprise unit goes through the process of self-transformation at its own pace.

Conclusion

"**D**IVIDING AN ELEPHANT IN HALF DOES NOT PRODUCE TWO SMALL EL-EPHANTS," states Peter Senge's tenth law of systems thinking. "Living systems have integrity. Their character depends on the whole. The same is true for organizations; to understand the most challenging managerial issues requires seeing the whole system that generates the issues," Senge elaborates on this law in his influential book *The Fifth Discipline* (Senge 1990). This explains why Stephen Spewak's division of enterprise architecture into four architecture domains—business architecture, data architecture, applications architecture, and technology architecture—led to the situation enterprise architecture professionals find themselves in today, hopelessly believing that if they master the parts, they will eventually master the whole.

A novel approach to enterprise architecture—the Alpha Architecture—maintains the conceptual integrity of the discipline by creating an overarching structure that can flexibly accommodate enterprise constructs of various types. The Alpha Architecture views the enterprise as a multilevel structure, where each level is implemented as a flat network of uniformly constructed entities.

The top enterprise level is implemented as a network of units of two types. Whereas specialist units satisfy needs and directly interact with consumers, executive units provide continuous feedback (set and adjust operational boundary conditions) to specialist units and ensure that they make optimal contribution to the success of the whole. Specialist units coordinate their efforts using a lightweight, indirect coordination mechanism—Worknet Management—inspired by stigmergy, a coordination mechanism used by social insects.

Units are powerful sociocomputing constructs that encapsulate and create synergy between main (human and artificial agents), supporting (virtual assistants, tools, and objects in the Internet of Things), and enabling (infrastructure and platforms) computational components. If well-engineered and properly aligned, seven unit-design domains—purpose, function, process, structure, culture, storage, and memory—enable coherent delivery of unit offerings (products and services).

The Alpha Architecture transforms the enterprise in three phases. The first phase, differentiation, transforms the enterprise into a network of units and establishes unit boundaries. The next phase, integration, establishes indirect connectivity, communication, and coordination between the units. During the last phase, reengineering, each unit transforms itself at its own pace.

FREQUENTLY ASKED QUESTIONS

Q: **What is the scope of enterprise architecture?**
Enterprise architecture abstracts the complexity related to manufacturing activities in order to focus on *computation*.

Q: **What are the relations between enterprise architecture and other architectural disciplines?**
Enterprise architecture depends on and must align with the *organization (social) architecture* of the enterprise. This means that the

enterprise must be architected as a social system, not as a manufacturing or computation system.

Q: How does the enterprise perform computation?
Computation is performed by agents, agent assistants, tools, things, platforms, and infrastructure. Agents—human and artificial—are considered *independent computational building blocks*; assistants, tools, and things are considered *supporting computational building blocks*; and platforms and infrastructure are *enabling computational building blocks*.

Q: How does the enterprise organize computational activities?
Organization architecture partitions the enterprise into organization *units*, which enterprise architecture considers *advanced computational building blocks*. All other computational blocks are logically encapsulated within units so that every computational asset is owned by one and only one unit.

Q: What does the enterprise look like?
The enterprise is a *network* of interrelated *units*. Each unit establishes *relations* with other units and entities in the surrounding *environment*. These include organizational relations (directing/reporting), collaborative relations (coordination, information sharing), compliance relations (with regulatory bodies), economic relations (an exchange of offerings for money or other types of value), and other types of relations.

Q: How can I construct an enterprise?
Constructing the enterprise is a two-step process: (1) construct units and (2) integrate the units. The combined external boundaries of constituent units comprise the boundary of the enterprise.

Q: What are the types of units?

There are two types of units: *executive units* and *specialist units*. Each executive unit ensures that units under its authority contribute their best to the whole entity that the executive unit represents. Unlike executive units, specialist units do not have units under their authority.

Q: Does an enterprise have other parts in addition to units?

No, the unit is the only type of enterprise-level building block. All other computational building blocks are encapsulated within units.

Q: How do I integrate units?

Three types of integration agents—connectivity agents (mediators), communication agents (intermediators), and coordination agents—are created and encapsulated within each executive unit. These agents connect, coordinate, and enable communication between units under their authority and entities in the environment.

Q: What does a unit look like?

A unit is a bounded network of human and artificial agents. The agents are supported by assistants and are equipped with tools. In order to operate, artificial agents, virtual assistants, and tools require computational platforms and infrastructure.

Q: How can I construct a unit?

A unit is constructed of the following modules: structure, boundary, storage, and memory. Building the structure module involves the construction of human and artificial agents, their assistants, and their required tools. The boundary module consists of facades, which serve as containers for interfaces—web applications, mobile apps, services, microservices, APIs, and so on. The storage and memory modules can be implemented as combinations of warehouses, databases, file systems, reporting suites, and so forth.

Q: What is the role of a unit in the enterprise?
Every unit creates a unique unifying business context for every agent and other enterprise computational asset.

References

Ackoff, Russell L. 2010. *Differences That Make a Difference: An Annotated Glossary of Distinctions Important in Management.* Axminster, Devon: Triarchy Press.

Alexander, Christopher. 2002. *The Nature of Order: An Essay on the Art of Building and the Nature of the Universe, Book 1: The Phenomenon of Life.* Berkeley: Center for Environmental Structure.

Alfnes, Erlend. 2008. *Enterprise Reengineering: A Strategic Framework and Methodology.* Germany: VDM Verlag Dr. Müller.

Brooks Jr., Frederick P. 1995. *The Mythical Man-Month: Essays on Software Engineering.* Anniversary Edition. Boston: Addison-Wesley Professional.

Erikson, Erik H. 1993. *Childhood and Society.* New York: W. W. Norton & Company.

Fayol, Henri. 1917. *Administration Industrielle et Générale ; prévoyance, organisation, commandement, coordination, controle.* Paris: H. Dunod et E. Pinat.

Forrester, Jay W. 1998. *Designing the Future.* Address given at Universidad de Sevilla, Sevilla, Spain.

Foster, Richard N., and Sarah Kaplan. 2001. *Creative Destruction: Why Companies That Are Built to Last Underperform the*

Market, and How to Successfully Transform Them. New York: Currency/Doubleday.

"Gartner Predicts over 70 Percent of Global 2000 Organisations Will Have at Least One Gamified Application by 2014." 2011. Press release. Gartner.

Goldin, Dina, and David Keil. 2005. "Interactive Models for Design of Software-Intensive Systems." Paper presented at Foundations of Interactive Computation 2005. Edinburgh.

Grasse, P. P. 1959. "La reconstruction du nid et les coordinations interindividuelles chez Bellicositermes natalensis et Cubitermes." *Insectes Sociaux* 6: 41–81.

Hammer, Michael, and James Champy. 1993. *Reengineering the Corporation: A Manifesto for Business Revolution.* New York, NY: Harper Business.

Henderson, Rebecca M., and Kim B. Clark. 1990. "Architectural Innovation: The Reconfiguration of Existing Product Technologies and the Failure of Established Firms." *Administrative Science Quarterly.*

Heylighen, Francis. 2015. *Stigmergy as a Universal Coordination Mechanism: Components, Varieties and Applications.* New York: Springer.

Hohpe, Gregor, and Bobby Woolf. 2003. *Enterprise Integration Patterns: Designing, Building, and Deploying Messaging Solutions.* Boston: Addison-Wesley Professional.

Lindberg, C. A. 2012. *Oxford American Writer's Thesaurus.* 3rd ed. New York: Oxford University Press.

Lissack, Michael, and Johan Roos. 2000. *The Next Common Sense: Mastering Corporate Complexity through Coherence.* London: Nicholas Brealey Publishing.

Marz, Nathan, with James Warren. 2015. *Big Data: Principles and Best Practices of Scalable Realtime Data Systems*. Shelter Island, NY: Manning Publications.

Mintzberg, Henry. *Managing*. 2009. San Francisco: Berrett-Koehler Publishers.

Mitleton-Kelly, Eve. 2003. *Complex Systems and Evolutionary Perspectives of Organisations: The Application of Complexity Theory to Organisations*. Bingley: Emerald Group Publishing.

Osterman Research. 2009. *Comparing the Cost of Email Systems*. http://www.ostermanresearch.com/whitepapers/or_nov0509.pdf.

Paharia, Rajat. 2013. *Loyalty 3.0: How to Revolutionize Customer and Employee Engagement with Big Data and Gamification*. New York: McGraw-Hill Education.

Sayles, Leonard R. 1979. *Leadership: What Effective Managers Really Do…and How They Do It*. New York: McGraw-Hill.

Senge, Peter M. 1990. *The Fifth Discipline: The Art & Practice of the Learning Organization*. New York, NY: Doubleday Currency.

Sessions, Roger. 2007. Interview with John Zachman. *Perspectives of the International Association of Software Architects*. http://www.zachman.com/images/ZI_PIcs/rogersessionsinterview.pdf.

Simon, Herbert A. 1962. "The Architecture of Complexity." *Proceedings of the American Philosophical Society* 106 (6): 467–482.

Spewak, Steven H. 1993. *Enterprise Architecture Planning: Developing a Blueprint for Data, Applications, and Technology*. Hoboken: Wiley.

Suh, Nam P. 2001. *Axiomatic Design: Advances and Applications*. New York: Oxford University Press.

Theraulaz, G., and E. Bonabeau. 1999. "A Brief History of Stigmergy." *Artificial Life* 5: 97–116.

Van Dyke Parunak, H. 2006. "A Survey of Environments and Mechanisms for Human-Human Stigmergy" in *Environments for Multi-Agent Systems II.* Edited by D. Weyns, H. Van Dyke Parunak, and F. Michel. Berlin: Springer.

Wikipedia, The Free Encyclopedia, s.v. 2017. "Abstraction Layer," accessed January 20, 2017, https://en.wikipedia.org/wiki/Abstraction_layer.

WikiWikiWeb. 2014. "One More Level of Indirection," accessed January 20, 2017, http://wiki.c2.com/?OneMoreLevelOfIndirection.

Yegge, Steve. 2011. "Stevey's Google Platforms Rant." https://plus.google.com.

Zachman, John. 2015. "Defining Enterprise Architecture: The Systems Are the Enterprise." www.zachman.com (blog). Accessed Nov. 9, 2015. https://www.zachman.com/resources/zblog/item/defining-enterprise-architecture-the-systems-are-the-enterprise.

www.ingramcontent.com/pod-product-compliance
Lightning Source LLC
Chambersburg PA
CBHW052148070326
40689CB00050B/2516